Dear Mar

Sorry abo

Spelling!

SINGING WORDS

Happy Singing

Happy Christmas

Love

Sue x

SINGING WORDS

M. C. Newberry

JANUS PUBLISHING COMPANY
London, England

Janus Publishing Company Ltd,
105-107 Gloucester Place,
London W1U 6BY

www.januspublishing.co.uk

British Library Cataloguing-in-Publication Data
A catalogue record for this book is available
from the British Library

ISBN 1 85756

Cover Design:

Printed and bound in Great Britain

Singing Words
M. C. Newberry

This entrancing collection of verse and lyrics reflects on life with a lightness of touch which makes reading each poem seem like experiencing a waft of fresh air. There is a clarity of expression that belies the deeply felt emotions that the works encompass.

M. C. Newberry writes of the beauty of the English countryside, of the passage of time and growing old, of loves loved and lost, of wartime memories and brave friends.

Throughout this collection the writer's insight cuts through the "insulation" of modern living and reveals the heart of the matter – whether he is discussing what he sees in the world around him or feelings closer to home. This inspiring volume will leave the reader wanting to constantly dip into its pages to reread many favourites.

Contents

The Galmpton Robin

The robin sang his song to me,
When I walked out by Galmpton Quay.
Alone he sang at twilight's gleam
Beside the darkening Devon stream.

I am life, his sweet song said,
An angel's voice above my head.
Exulting in his melody,
The robin sang his song for me.

The tiny song-bird touched my heart,
That day beside the dreaming Dart.
My spirit soared as I passed by
And joined the robin in the sky.

The robin red-breast will I seek
That sings his song by Galmpton Creek,
And sang his song of joy to me
When I walked out by Galmpton Quay.

George Best
Football Legend

Fame is such a fickle dame,
That in her clasp who would dare claim
To stay the same?

Like love, Time holds fame in its hand,
And cruelly pours away the strand
Of golden sand.

The wise man smiles and winks an eye,
And nods to bid his time goodbye,
Not asking why.

But skill, like art, survives the years,
Evoking joy and countless cheers,
And grateful tears.

It lives within the living breast
Of anyone who was a guest
At the feast of football from the Best.

Down by The Mewstone
A Walk to the River Dart Estuary

Near Kingswear Town, there stands a tree
That stands alone and waits for me
To take the track back to the sea,
The way down by The Mewstone.

Past the beacon in the corn,
Built for every seaman born,
To the works of war forlorn
At bay down by The Mewstone.

Above the rocks, beneath the pine,
Look-outs lost in leaf and vine,
Still staring out in dark design,
Decay down by The Mewstone.

When life and living make no sense
And all I care for gives offence,
I do not fret but get me hence
To stray down by The Mewstone.

And when I walk that winding lane
Towards the sea beyond the grain,
I find my peace of mind again –
And pray down by The Mewstone.

The fields my church, the wind my choir,
The sky above a mighty spire
That soars and draws my spirit higher
Each day down by The Mewstone.

Love Taught Me

I was the one who knew everything,
Had a "Bachelor of Loving" Degree;
Now I find that I know nothing
That matters a nickel to me.

I was the one who lost everything,
Got a "Loser in Loving" Degree;
Love taught me and now I've got nothing
That matters a nickel to me.

So listen up, don't be a know-all,
Don't think that you've got it made;
Be wise and beware of this warning
Or your chances of loving will fade:
Never think that you know everything,
Or degree by bitter degree,
You'll hear yourself say:
"I've got nothing
That matters a nickel to me."

I was the one who wasn't listening
To what love was saying, you see;
Now I find that I hear nothing
That matters a nickel to me.

I was the one who wasn't watching
When love waved goodbye and went free,
And now I find that I see nothing
That matters a nickel to me.

I was the one who had everything
But degree by bitter degree,
Love taught me and now I've got nothing
That matters a nickel to me.

Love taught me and now I've got no one
That matters a nickel to me.

Once Upon A Time

Once Upon A Time
We had this magic thing called love;
It shone into our lives
Just like the stars above.
And with the stars came heaven too,
But storytellers know,
Once Upon A Time was long ago.

Once Upon A Time
Love was happy ever after;
In a word – eternity,
Filled with joy and laughter.
Love was always – love was true,
But little children know,
Once Upon A Time was long ago.

Young and carefree, you and me,
Love was all that we could see,
So happy that it met us.
Thrilling us [illegible] heart and mind,
Never dreaming th[illegible]'d find
How soon it would forge[illegible].

Once Upon A Time
Love had a happy ending;
Love would not forsake us,
No fake and no pretending.
Love was real, me and you – but
How soon we were to know…
Once Upon A Time was long ago.

The Property Developer

What care I for gate or fence?
Come let us talk of pounds and pence.

What care I for trees and fields?
Pray tell me what the profit yields.

What care I for bird or beast?
(Unless the creatures are deceased.)

What care I for the vocal majority
When I've got the ear of the local authority?

And I always see as heaven sent
Congenial chums in Parliament.

I'm grateful enough to make sure I select a
Retiring MP as a company director.

A Distant Haze

Wood smoke, the good smoke,
Drifting through the trees,
Brings the haze of other days
And childhood memories.

Wood scent, the good scent,
Pungent and sublime,
Brings to mind the yearning kind
Of youth that envies time.

Flame glow, the same glow
As passion's rich red rose,
Sight and scent by nature meant
When youth to adult grows.

Remembrance Day

Young man – see them marching by,
Their medals catch the light.
Look and hold your head up high,
You'll see no finer sight.

Old men passing in their pride
Were once as young as you.
Now, as then, they're side by side
But now they're growing few.

Should one chance to catch your eye,
Young man, don't look away.
For your tomorrow, live or die,
They gave you their today.

In The Night

When darkness comes to call
And finds me on my own now,
I turn my face against the wall,
So sad and so alone now.

Why can't it be the way –
The way it was before?
I thought you'd always stay,
How could I be so sure?
But now I wonder why
I wouldn't see the score...

In the night
When you were by my side,
In the night,
It hurt so how you cried
In the night.

When you walked out on me
I said you'd soon surrender,
This selfish fool just couldn't see
That love was just a lender.

Why can't it be the way –
The way it was before?
I go from day to day,
I've gone from rich to poor,
And love has said goodbye
Till you walk in my door...

In the night,
So strange now how I see –
In the night,
Babe, hurry back to me
In the night.

An Anthem For Gibraltar

Between two seas you proudly keep
The key to Europe's gate;
Old guardian of the ocean deep
That watches o'er the Strait.

Mighty Rock – the sword and gun
You've seen, and felt the flame.
When underneath the timeless sun
The mighty warlords came.

Gibraltarians – with one voice
Stand firm upon your shore;
Look to the future and rejoice:
Gibraltar evermore!

In centuries past the clash of arms
Swept round your mountain brow
That tells of victories and alarms
And calls upon us now.

Forward to your destiny,
Secure in friends well made;
Your place assured in history,
Can tunes of glory fade?

Gibraltarians – with one voice
Stand firm upon your shore;
Look to the future and rejoice:
Gibraltar evermore!

Many races…many creeds
Have walked your ancient walls;
Famous faces…famous deeds,
Gibraltar now recalls.

To the future now we gaze,
As here in peace we pray,
In hope of even better days,
Gibraltar – here we stay.

Gibraltarians – stand – sing out!
In pride at freedom's door;
Give thanks and let the bells ring out
Gibraltar evermore!

Gibraltarians – with one voice
Stand firm upon your shore;
Look to the future and rejoice:
Gibraltar evermore!

Thoughts At Christmas

How fitting now in deep December,
When days are short and life is low,
That in our hearts we will remember
Those we loved who had to go.

Christmas hours are briefly bright,
Their spark is spent in winter's pay
And soon surrenders to the night,
When light, like life, goes on its way.

But O how wonderful this living!
How magical this life we own,
That God gives us to go on giving
When He takes those that we have known.

Yesterday Once More

Pausing high above the beach,
I watch the children out of reach,
Racing down the golden sand,
Leaping...laughing...hand in hand.

Children dancing in the sea
Remind me how I used to be,
Free from care, fizzing with fun,
A happy boy beneath the sun.

Time goes by, yet time stands still,
And moment follows moment till
What is now once went before
And what is past returns once more.

I watch the children in the sea
And when I laugh, they laugh with me,
And when they shout, I shout with joy!
Again I am that happy boy.

Hawk

Keen-eyed keeper of the skies,
Lord of everything that flies,
There's no way your daily prey
Will wait to pass the time of day.

Patrolling country, cliff and city,
You were not designed for pity;
Not for you the hurting heart,
You were born a breed apart.

Nature fashioned hawk and prey
To keep the balance nature's way;
Not for you to reason why
One must live and one must die.

I Should Have Called You

So sad and so alone now,
So lonely on my own now,
I realize that I was mean to you;
So foolish and so blind then,
I find now that I mind when
I've grown so wise
And mean to love anew.

I should have called you
When you were all alone,
I should have called you –
Just picked up the phone.
I would have told you how I loved you…
How I'd care for you;
I could have let my heart
Speak all the love
It dared for you.

I should have called you
And said I love you so;
I should have called you,
Instead I let you go.
And now I sit alone
and shed a lonely tear,
I should have called you, my dear.

I should have called you,
To say I'd be around;
I should have told you
Of all this love I've found;
I would have whispered

All the things
That this heart feels inside
I could have shown you
That there's nowhere left
For them to hide.

I should have called you
So you'd be sure to know;
I should have called you,
Instead I let you go.
And tho' your phone is ringing
I get no reply
And now I call you and cry.

The Country Singer

I loved to drive to the old songs
On the radio each day;
They said the things I felt myself,
And sure wished I could play.

One day I met a wise man
Who read me clear right through;
He said *"You ought to learn, son,*
That's what you ought to do.

Hear that radio when you ride
But listen to what I say...
You could sing of what's inside
If you learnt how to play.

No guy needs a nanny
To learn to play pianny;
If you can drive a hot rod car,
You could drive a hot guitar."

He left me with this parting pearl
Of wisdom on his way –
I won't forget his goodbye words
Until my dying day.

"It's just a case of wanting, son,
How much and just how bad
You need to let that music tell
The thoughts you've always had.

Hear that radio when you ride,
But listen to what I say;
You could sing of what's inside
If you learnt how to play."

I bless that wise man from the past
Whose words I won't forget;
The way he read me clear right through
The moment that we met.

"Hear that radio when you ride,
But listen to what I say;
You could sing of what's inside
If you learnt how to play."

Now I love to drive to the new songs
On the radio each day,
And I hear my songs sing back to me,
And hear my fingers play.

The Gay Dog

I like a handsome hound for sport,
But a pretty pup's my treasure;
The hound will stretch and not be caught,
My pup will stretch with pleasure.

The hound will bare his teeth at me
If I should dare to scold him;
My pup will bare his soul to me
When I reach out and hold him.

Proud before my bed at night,
The handsome hound ignores me;
My pup waits till I dim the light
Then lies down and adores me.

I like a handsome hound for fun,
But a pretty pup's my treasure;
The hound will take his chance to run,
My pup will take his pleasure.

My London

In all the world, there's nowhere quite
Like London on a soft spring night,
When saffron sunset sends its grace
To linger on a much-loved face.

And all around, the very air
Thrills with time, as if aware
That this great city is the stage
For this and every other age.

So much history, so much done,
So much to tell the setting sun.

Question

It is not the way of Man
To look upon each day,
And do the very best he can,
And do it while he may?

They Say

They say that the first day of spring
Brings the chance now:
It brings you the chance of romance.
They say new attractions will lead
you a dance now...
But all you recall is her glance.

They say that the girl who just
upped and departed,
And left you alone with your pain,
Could run back to you
While you're still broken-hearted
And give you her love once again.

All you know is she's gone
But you still won't believe,
And chill winter creeps into your soul;
Your head says go on
But your heart says don't leave
When you see her wherever you stroll.

They say that the first day of spring
brings the chance now:
The chance of new love in the air.
They say a past love
Is a thing of the past now,
Remember, they say: *Life's not fair.*

Talkin' The Walk

Go on – walk away!
Should I beg you to stay
When you say
That you're leaving for good?

You've told me before…
Many times – and what's more –
I don't think you will,
Or you would.

Go on – if you dare!
Take that step down the stair
To the door
That leads out on the street

To a wide world that waits
While ours dis-in-te-grates,
And I still feel your warmth
On the sheet.

Go on – take a hike!
From this life you don't like,
I'm tired of you
Talkin' your talk.

Make your move from your man (gal)
Hit the road if you can (with no pal)
Or are you just
Talkin' the walk?

Memory

Memory, sweet memory,
That dwells within the heart of me,
Why is it that the things I see
Are not the things that used to be?

Did I walk those wild wood ways
Of make believe and childhood plays
That *once upon a time* portrays?
Did I really live those days?

The faces that I used to know,
The places where I used to go,
Now, like the tide, ebb to and fro,
Was it ever really so?

Memory, sweet memory,
Why do I doubt your constancy?
Is it that my dreams and me
Live life as we would have it be?

Dambuster

Dedicated to Sqdn Ldr G. L. Johnson DFC
(Bomb-aimer – 617 "Dambuster" Squadron)

Whippet lean and dry of tone,
With manner self-effacing,
He conjured up the distant drone
Of bombers moonlight chasing.

He made it easy to believe
How different were those days when
Young men like him dared to achieve
Great deeds in daring ways then.

Though many springs had left behind
That distant May-moon night,
Those who listened would soon find
Themselves aboard that flight.

In the moon-bright ray a life away
From the mocking and modern world,
He and we lay in the bomb-aimer's bay
As the target beneath us unfurled.

Time and around, and around yet again,
The hazards and risks multiplying,
Till the right time arrived and the Lancaster
Dived at the target for which it was trying.

A hit but no breach, then away out of reach,
The hand that was held had been played;
No more could be done but much had been won,
While sacrifice was sought – and was made.

When God wants for angels (and He wants the best)
To safeguard the Kingdom of Heaven,
There are many deserving but may I suggest
The squadron they call six one seven.

In Memoriam

The Queen Mother Remembered

The Lantern has gone from the lighthouse,
The Candle has flickered and died,
But the spirit will always shine brightly,
In courage and duty and pride.

The guiding Light's gone from the gatehouse,
The comfort and warmth disappear,
But whenever we think on that century
The marvellous memories bring cheer.

The Beacon alight in God's bright house,
The Candle is flaring above,
While those memories will find us forever,
In lightness and laughter and love.

Morning Comes

Morning comes but once a day,
And that's enough for me,
I face each day without you,
Making do with misery.

Morning comes but once a day,
And with it comes the light
To show me what I see so well:
That there's no end in sight...to my

Suffering, hard suffering, without you,
Why, oh why did this fool ever doubt you?
So beautiful and so wise
With love's ache deep in your eyes,
And now I ache for everything about you.

Morning comes but once a day,
My punishment goes on,
For all the ways I hurt you
In the dark days dead and gone.

Morning comes but once a day,
But that's enough for me,
I face each day without you,
Making do with misery – and my

Suffering, hard suffering, without you,
Why, oh why did this fool ever doubt you?
So beautiful and so wise
With love's sigh deep in your eyes,
And now I sigh for everything about you.

Morning comes but once a day,
I close my eyes and try
To wash away the memory
Of when you went and why.

Morning comes but once a day,
And that's enough for me,
I face each day without you,
Making do with misery.

What Do I Know?

She said it was over between us,
She told me that I had to go;
Her ideal affair didn't mean us –
I asked myself: "What do I know?"

She said she'd found love with another,
She told me she couldn't say no;
That I was just like a big brother –
I asked myself: "What do I know?"

Love and longing go hand in hand,
And pride and passion join the band
When daydreams don't pan out as planned.
Then nightmares haunt the hopeless case
And soon the jealous phantoms chase
All chance of happiness into space.

She said she was brimming with pity,
She told me she knew I was low;
Trying to be worldly and witty –
I asked myself: "What do I know?"

She said that we shouldn't feel sorrow,
She boasted about her new beau;
Now I'm marrying a millionairess tomorrow –
I ask myself: "What do I know?"

Bore

How odd there's no law
Against being a bore;
You're so sure in your core
That there could be.

When you're stuck with a bore
Exercising his jaw
Right next door, you're so sure
That there should be!

Streaps Bothy
Remembering a Walking Holiday in Scotland

Misty, come the memories
Of long departed days,
Reminding me of happy times
Spent walking highland ways;
Distant mountain silhouettes
Like giants stand and stare,
To tell me that I've long since left
But they're still waiting there.

The images of those I knew.
I see in my mind's eye.
They pass before me even now
As then they passed me by –
Ghosts now in that wild place –
There's nothing to be seen,
No sound of laughter, talk of friends,
To mark where I have been.

Last Post

There's this to say for getting old:
You take more care against the cold,
And value each new day.

And this to say for getting old:
You want to keep, and not to scold,
The children at their play.

And this to say for getting old:
It's always welcome to be told
To take a seat and stay.

And this to say for getting old:
You may not be so brash and bold,
But still you have your say.

There's this to say for getting old,
With silver threads among the gold,
And loved ones gone away.

At least you got to getting old!
And when at last life loses hold,
Salute and draw your pay.

It's Not Enough

It's not enough to think it,
You have to tell me that you care;
Tell me every livelong day
And love will find me there.

It's not enough to tell me,
You have to show me that you're mine;
Show me that it's no cliché
And love will surely shine.

It's not enough to show me,
You have to be with me to stay;
Be with me for evermore
And love will light the way.

So many people trying
But they seldom make it last;
So many with no future
And an unforgiving past –

Heartbroken and heartbreakers
With the cruel clock chasing fast …
Never let the chance of love go sighing,
Never let the chance of love go crying …

Always chase the chance of love undying.

Until I Saw Your Face

I never knew what love looked like
Until I saw your face;
I never knew what life could be
Until I found your grace.

I didn't care that love wasn't there,
What you don't have you don't miss;
I didn't know what it was to share
The commitment in your kiss.

But I see now that I was searching
All the time and every place,
But I never knew what love looked like
Until I saw your face.

The world is full of people thronging,
Perhaps not always wise;
Everyone is looking and longing
For that light in someone's eyes.
But sometimes it's too deep inside,
Disguised by hurt and need,
To give it words stripped clean of pride
For other hearts to read.

I never knew what love looked like
Until I saw your face;
I never knew what life could be
Until I found your grace.

I didn't mind that I didn't find
What other hearts hungered for;
Love was a caller disinclined
To come knocking at my locked door.

But I see now that I was searching
All the time and every place,
But I never knew what love looked like
Until I saw your face.

My Mother

It's a while now since she passed away,
And time has hurried on,
But still I hear her softly say
"You'll miss me when I'm gone".

With each and every passing day
I sadly think upon
Those quiet words I heard her say:
"You'll miss me when I'm gone".

The Death Of Persian Punch
The Going Down Of The Sun

Brave eyes wept at the Ascot course
When he came to the end of his run;
For the going down of that great horse
Was like the going down of the sun.

Brilliantly, he had brought the light
Into so many days,
And now he'd fought his final fight
Before their grief-filled gaze.

But when the sun comes up each dawn
To ease the troubled heart.
We will recall the heart that was born
And beat in a horse apart.

What's The Use?

Some people covet honours,
Others wealth and fame;
But what's the use?
When life cuts loose
We all end up the same!

Make Your Mind Up

Make your mind up if you want me,
Tell me now or let me go;
Can't you show what's in your heart,
That's all I want to know.

Make your mind up if you need me,
To be there right by your side;
Just say the words I long to hear
And say goodbye to pride.

Make your mind up if you love me,
Show me that your heart is true;
This man has made his mind up –
And this man's in love with you.

Why do people rarely say
The things they really mean?
Why use words fit for the birds…
Why don't they just come clean?
Think of all the heartache
When love itself is through;
Best to say without delay:
My darling – I love you.

Be Grateful For The Dark Days

Be grateful for the dark days,
And when one comes along
Why waste your time in wondering
Just where it all went wrong?

Be grateful for the dark days,
And when one comes in sight,
Don't devote time despairing
If things will turn out right.

Be grateful for the dark days,
They're made to make you glad
When everything about them
Makes you think you should feel bad.

Folk will always seek the sun,
It helps a soul feel good,
Who'd have sunshine every day
Even if they could?
We need the darker side of life
To make us strong, I guess,
And help us all appreciate
Our lives when we have less.

Be grateful for the dark days,
The dark days are soon past;
They come to help remind us
That the worst times never last.

Be grateful for the dark days,
They lead you to the rest;
As sure as night gives way to day,
They guide you to the best.

Be grateful for the dark days
That bring you to the bright;
Why waste your time in worrying
When you're led towards the light?

Sunday Song

Sunday always seems to be
The day my thoughts go flying free,
And times gone by return to me,
From yesterday.

A Sunday street's a bygone street
That echoes someone else's feet,
And other voices soft and sweet,
From yesterday.

A Sunday bell's a timeless knell
That tolling has a tale to tell,
And chiming casts a magic spell,
From yesterday.

Sunday is the day I find
That brings back times left far behind,
To fill and thrill the willing mind,
From yesterday.

English Hills

Our English hills like sentries stand,
Proud guardians of an ancient land.
Across their brows, God, ever wise,
Has draped the everchanging skies.

While in their valleys, gently laid,
There lie the things that man has made,
Briefly come and quickly gone
To dust as English hills look on.

Long they've stood and long will last,
Mute witnesses to ages past,
Of other days and other men
Our English hills won't see again.

Look upon them...silent...still,
Yet listen closely and you will
Be sure to hear them softly say
"In time you go; in time we stay".

The Primrose

Peeping from beneath the tree,
The lemon primrose spoke to me.
Winter's done, I heard it say,
Warmer days are on their way.

Mother Nature waits on me
(*The First Rose* is my name, you see)
While other flowers stay in bed,
I welcome spring and show my head.

Then, with the golden daffodil,
I gild the countryside until
In turn, the other blooms appear,
Assured that summer's lease is near.

Peeping from beneath the tree,
I heard the primrose speak to me.
When nature lives her life anew,
You'll hear the primrose speak to you.

Take Me Back To Rock And Roll

Take me back to Rock and Roll,
To that music in my soul,
To the music that was ours
When we were young.

It hasn't left me yet,
Gee babe, how could I forget
Any Rock and Roll song
That was sung?

Take me back to Blueberry Hill,
Fats sure knew how to thrill,
To Buddy and The Crickets'
"Peggy Sue",

With Chuck and Jerry Lee,
That's where I want to be,
And I know darling,
That's what you want too.

Three Steps to Heaven take me there,
I'm Walking free from care,
C'mon Everybody,
It's So Fine.

Say Mama, You're Sixteen,
At The Hop – A Teenage Queen,
And I'm Dreaming
Of Love Potion Number Nine.

Please Be My Guest and Stay,
Here you've got love Everyday,
And we've got Rock and Roll
And it ain't done.

Yeah – That'll Be The Day,
Girl, we'll Not Fade Away.
Rock and Roll is
Still the number one.

Made In Heaven

Verse 1 – Love Match
Your love is made in heaven
For all the world to see;
My love is made in heaven,
So you and I make "we";
You've a place
And I've a place
(I only hope God's got the space!)
A love match made in heaven,
That's how it's going to be.

Verse 2 – Marriage
Each girl's a bride in heaven,
And every man a groom;
A marriage made in heaven
Survives the doom and gloom;
Each girl a bride
Each guy a groom
(I only hope God's got the room!)
A marriage made in heaven,
That's how it's going to be.

Verse 3 – Family
One and one in heaven,
That means me and you;
But it's even more like heaven
When adding one to two; and
Adding one to two gets three
The way to start a family
(I like to think God will agree!)
A family made in heaven,
That's how it's going to be.

A future made in heaven,
Made for you and me.

George Lloyd
– Composer –
Dedicated during his lifetime

Muse, whose music spans the years
And brings forth unaccustomed tears,
You follow still your lonely star
And let not fickle fashion mar

Your joyful message to mankind
That grateful hearts will gladly find.
Be not discouraged in your art,
Be not dissuaded from your part.

Faithful muse, the light is near,
See the darkness disappear;
Your day is near, the night is past,
Your time has come, at last…at last.

The Spider

Threadbare though his home may be,
The spider doesn't mind;
He takes to tea the passing flea
And others of his kind.

The spider can be found on line,
A host beyond compare;
He's always having guests to dine,
His larder's seldom bare.

He likes to welcome company by
To watch his skill at weaving;
But when they think it's time to fly,
They find it awkward leaving.

He spins his yarn for those that missed
Detecting each distraction;
Alas for them, he can't resist
Their edible attraction.

Sunset Over Start Bay
("Exercise Tiger" Remembered)

Sunset slowly trims its lamp
Beyond the Start Bay Light,
And dayglow fades before the shades
Of fast approaching night.

The sky of blue's a darker hue,
And soft now sings the lark,
When through the clouds,
Like billowing shrouds,
The moonglow makes its mark.

Across the bay, the Start Point Ray
Flashes – clear and bright –
And brings to mind
A different kind...
A dangerous kind of light.

Of flares, and ships caught unawares,
Shells bursting in the ears;
Of noise-filled night
Soon searing white
Above a sea of tears.

The Channel tide where brave men died
Still weeps upon the shore,
And in the gloom
Above their tomb,
The Dead rise up once more.

The ghostly Host embrace the coast
And share that shadowed strand;
Beyond life's lease,
In love and peace,
The Dead stand hand in hand.

As moonlight spills on Devon hills,
And silent sinks the lark,
The eternal star of the day
Makes way
For the eternal stars of the dark.

I Get Memories

I get memories of our melody
Before it went off song;
I get dreams as night
That hurt me right
Where your heart should belong;
I get letters from your lawyer,
And your Ma and Papa too,
But I never get a letter from you.

Serves me right for trusting love
The way a sucker can (alt. But I was in a whirl)
And thinking that was all I had to do;
Serves me right for being
Such a trusting kind of man (alt. girl)
And thinking love was meant
For me and you.

I get heartache from remembering
The way it all went wrong;
I get pain inside
From my hurt pride
At being strung along;
I get phone calls from your lawyer,
And your Ma and Papa too,
But I never get a phone call from you.

Serves me right for trusting love
The way a sucker can (alt. But I was in a whirl)
And thinking that was all I had to do;
Serves me right for being
Such a trusting kind of man (alt. girl)
And thinking love was meant
For me and you.

I get lonesome on my ownsome
And I miss you every day;
I get crazy mad
And soulful sad
And love you, come what may;
I get visits from your lawyer,
And your Ma and Papa too,
But I never get a visit from you.

I Love You Today

Lucky it's me –
So glad it's you,
Enchantment in all
Of the things that we do,
My feelings are many,
My words but a few:
Remember – I love you today.

Sometimes, it's right,
Sometimes, it's wrong,
Sometimes our tune
Is a now and then song,
I'll say it again
Like I've said all along:
Remember – I love you today.

The smile that I know
The way you say hello,
The thrill that I get
When we kiss;
The ache in my heart
That begins when we part,
All the things about you
That I miss.

Maybe we could –
Maybe we would
Always be tender,
It's good that we should;
When love comes so rarely
It's misunderstood:
Remember – I love you today.

Sometimes, it's joy,
Sometimes, it's pain,
Always the sun
Coming after the rain,
And always I'll tell you
Again and again:
Remember – I love you today.

Be Still

Be still, my heart, my breath, my mind,
Be still and leave all grief behind.
Be still beyond this mortal air,
Be still in God's immortal care.

Denis Compton
Final Innings

The heroes are all going now,
And we are left to grieve;
A fond farewell – a final bow,
Too soon they take their leave.

Those bright-eyed boys of yesterday,
The best of bygone years,
Now stride a starry field of play
To everlasting cheers.

But we still see them in their prime
Beneath an English sky,
Stepping out, untouched by time,
Immortals do not die.

Still The Flowers Grow

When nights are long and spirits low,
Remember – still the flowers grow.

When days are short and full of woe,
Remember – still the flowers grow.

When health and wealth ebb to and fro,
Remember – still the flowers grow.

When friends and family come and go,
Remember – still the flowers grow.

When life has little left to show,
Remember – still the flowers grow.

I Saw Her Walk In

I was feeling so low, didn't know which way to go
When I saw her walk in through the door
She looked straight at me like I was all she could see
And I floated clear up from the floor.

Her gaze held my eyes like the stars in the skies
I've never felt anything so strong
The other guys stared and I was feeling so scared
Could it be I was reading things wrong?

It wasn't that far from the door to the bar
But it seemed like a mile to me
Then she stood by my side just like some sweet bride
As the band started earning their fee.

She ordered a drink while I tried hard to think
Of something real smart I could say
Then her beer appeared while the audience cheered
And I prayed hard she wouldn't walk away.

Then she pressed real close there right under my nose
And said "Haven't we met before?"
I stuttered, went red, couldn't believe that I said
"If we had, I'd remember for sure."

Her blush was a thrill that remains with me still
As she said with a quiet kind of smile
"I hope you don't mind but I think that I'd kind
of enjoy being here for a while."

Now we two are wed and life's forging ahead
But we still go along to that bar
Where joy first began for shy girl and shy man
Used to looking at love from afar.

Daddy Knew Johnny Cash

I put a lot of sweat into the songs I wrote,
Every last word and every last note,
So it hurt when my Daddy would clear his throat,
And his eyes begin to flash.

"Where's the heart and the soul?" he'd say to me,
"Here's my advice and it's for free..."
And I'd get it all from Ay to Zee – but
Daddy knew Johnny Cash.

Oh, they weren't friends – or anything like,
Never met for a beer or went for a hike,
Never stood on a stage and shared a mike – but
Daddy knew Johnny Cash.

Knew every song the Man in Black wrote,
Every last word and every last note,
Could recite every one with a lump in his throat,
Yeah – Daddy knew Johnny Cash.

"The tune's not bad," he'd grudgingly say,
After he'd heard me sing and play,
"It's the person inside you that's wandered away",
Yeah – Daddy knew Johnny Cash.

Now when I get an idea for a song,
I invite my heart and soul along,
And when I do, I can't go wrong,
Yeah – Daddy knew Johnny Cash.

They've both gone on and that don't seem fair,
But they taught me that songs have to care,
And I'll bet up in that *Great Somewhere*
Daddy knows Johnny Cash.